A Friend's Kitchen
مطبخ الصديقة

'Al-Saddiq Al-Raddi's new book manages to be several things at once. It's certainly a political protestation, an act of resistance of the spirit to oppression in Sudan and to the pressures the UK places on political exiles. But it is at the same time an ecstatic, disorienting celebration of language and the imagination, and a raw, grieving set of eulogies to the loss of love, friendship and imaginative freedom ... We owe his translators a great debt, in that they manage successfully to convey what anyone who has heard him read knows is the dizzying rhetorical power and force of his Arabic.'
— W.N. Herbert, author of *The Wreck of the Fathership*

'This poetry collection sheds light on what it means to be a poet of the diaspora, being forced into exile from his native Sudan to his new home in London as a refugee. His powerful poetry of protest and hope, skillfully translated from Arabic by Bryar Bajalan with the poet Shook, offers the reader a unique view of the land and people that have suffered so much under the regime of Omar al-Bashir. It is a book filled with grief, beauty and love, enhanced by its power of denouncement. Al-Raddi's voice is an outstanding contribution not only to African poetry but to world poetry.'
— Leo Boix, author of *Ballad of a Happy Immigrant*

'A book to be entered rather than read. Emerging from a Dadaist-inspired stream-of-consciousness process of writing, these poems capture a mind moving through the lived moment, illuminated as though by a struck match. The lucid translation by Bajalan and Shook retains the beauty and integrity of the original, with poems that are clear-eyed, alive to grief and wonderment. Al-Raddi holds a mirror to the experience of living apart from family and home, and in doing so shows us we are not alone in our loneliness.'
— Shazea Quraishi, author of *The Glimmer*

'In this remarkable collection, grief and language move like water, like a force that cannot be contained. Al-Saddiq Al-Raddi's poetry brilliantly explores the ways in which community is fostered through the written word, and subsequently how the written word is fostered through community. Bryar Bajalan and Shook perform the graceful tightrope walk of translation, empowering Al-Raddi's words in a new language while containing the intention of their original script. This is a masterful collection, one that should be returned to again and again even as we toast our deaths and survive.'
— Aaron Kent, author of *The Working Classic*

Al-Saddiq Al-Raddi

A Friend's Kitchen

مطبخ الصديقة

Translated from Arabic by
Bryar Bajalan with the poet Shook

poetry
translation
centre

For Sarah Maguire and Hafiz Kheir

First published in 2023
by the Poetry Translation Centre Ltd
The Albany, Douglas Way, London, SE8 4AG

www.poetrytranslation.org

Poems © Al-Saddiq Al-Raddi 2012–2019
English Translations © Bryar Bajalan and Shook 2023
Introduction © Bryar Bajalan 2023
Afterword © Stephen Watts 2023

ISBN: 978-1-7398948-4-9

A catalogue record for this book is available from the British Library

Typeset in Minion by Poetry Translation Centre Ltd
and Adobe Arabic by WorldAccent Ltd

Series Editor: Erica Hesketh
Cover Design: Kit Humphrey
Printed in the UK by T.J. Books

The author and translators wish to thank the editors of the following publications, for publishing the following poems, sometimes in earlier versions: *Ambit*: 'What Is Your Name?!' / *Modern Poetry in Translation*: 'A Friend's Kitchen'

Special thanks, too, to Dr Rachel Dbeis, wonderful translator and dearest friend, particularly for her essential contributions to the translation of '121'. Thanks to Zêdan Xelef, Dr Alana Marie Levinson-LaBrosse and Dr Atef Alshaer for their generosity in reading and commenting on our translations. Thanks also to our editor Erica Hesketh.

The Poetry Translation Centre is supported using public funding by Arts Council England.

Supported using public funding by
ARTS COUNCIL ENGLAND
LOTTERY FUNDED

Contents

Introduction   6

What Is Your Name?!   12
A Friend's Kitchen   14
Female   16
I Miss You   18
Panic Attack   20
Tattoo   22
And You Don't Return to Me   24
The Book of Sorrows   26
121   28
The Aggressors   32
Asylum Papers   34
Queensway   38
Their Crowns   44
Homeless   46
Nearly Forgot You   48
My Corpse in the River   50
I Will Die on Wednesday!   54
No One!   56
From the Book of Erasure   58

Afterword   60

About the contributors   64

About the series   66

Introduction

I first met the Sudanese poet Al-Saddiq Al-Raddi in 2018 through my friend and co-translator Shook, when they were the Artist in Residence in Kashkul, the centre for art and culture at the American University of Iraq, Sulaimani, where I worked as a primary investigator and translator for three years. Initially, Shook and I worked on this translation project remotely with Al-Saddiq, who was based in London. Soon afterward I came to the UK to pursue a master's degree, and later doctorate, at the Institute of Arabic and Islamic Studies at the University of Exeter. This allowed me to work with Al-Saddiq more closely.

As I navigated my new life in the UK, I found I could relate to Al-Saddiq's poems in a more profound way; they helped me to make sense of my own exile experience. This was a time when I felt out of place and struggled with living abroad for the first time, trying hard to establish myself in this new soil. Al-Saddiq's poetry introduced me to the 'first cup of hot chocolate' that was as hot as 'the phone against my cheek on the other end, every night'. Al-Saddiq introduced me to my first winter, my first panic attack, and the number for the ambulance. He helped me re-remember after I 'mastered forgetting'. As he writes in 'Asylum Papers':

> You need roots to establish yourself in the soil
> Esoteric knowledge of petrology and the taxonomy of plants
> Reptilian species and the nature of the seasons
> The phyla of birds, etc.
>
> You need so much to be someone else.

*

Al-Saddiq was born in 1969 and grew up in Khartoum. He is the author of three collections of poetry and is considered one of Africa's greatest living poets writing in the Arabic language. From 2006, he was the cultural editor of the *Al-Sudani* newspaper, until he lost his position in July 2012 during the uprising against the dictatorship of Omar Al-Bashir. Al-Saddiq only escaped imprisonment that summer because, thanks to the miraculous timing of Poetry Parnassus (the world's largest ever gathering of international poets, at which Al-Saddiq represented Sudan), he was in the UK when a series of mass arrests took place. He successfully applied for asylum and has now lived in London for over a decade.

At great distance from his colleagues and publishers, Al-Saddiq began to use Facebook as a new medium to build bridges and reach his audience across continents. During the September 2019 uprising against Omar Al-Bashir's regime, Al-Saddiq published lively posts every day. Many of the poems featured in this collection were written for the uprising and were first published (in earlier versions) on Facebook. His output at that time ranged from protestations against the brutality of the regime and militia groups to eulogies for departed friends and everything that 'stimulates our will to live' – the ululations of mothers, the cooking on the street, the cheerful graffiti, incantations and prayers in the protest square (or, as Al-Saddiq calls it, 'the festival square').

Al-Saddiq composed these poems using a stream-of-consciousness technique designed to bypass his own self-censorship and judgement. Inspired by the Dadaists' collaborative fiction, Al-Saddiq intended for his process of writing and posting these poems to be collaborative, open to the public to share their ideas. While they were discussed online, the poems also circulated among supporters of the revolution, becoming rallying cries and signs to communicate their message.

Al-Saddiq's experiments with improvisational writing are grounded in an oral tradition of reciting Arabic poetry, and the poems themselves are steeped in Quranic language. His poetry has references and deep connections to Sufism, both in general and in its Sudanese manifestations. Like Ibn Al-Farid, Ibn Al-Arabi and Al-Hallaj, Al-Saddiq wraps his poetry in complex imagery to conceal his unorthodox beliefs. Of course, this didn't protect him from the same persecution endured by his Classical Sufi forebears. Al-Saddiq once told me that 'poetry is our failing attempts at relief'. In his case, these failed attempts are precisely crafted. He uses deceptively simple language to convey deep concepts that transport the reader to a simultaneously spiritual, exhausting, and relieving trance-like state.

*

In his poem 'The Book of Sorrows', Al-Saddiq illustrates the difficulties of living in exile and being exposed to new culture and a new way of life. In the poem he writes, 'It was my first winter in the darkness of the small room near the big train station; the bustling of late-night workers coloured my lonely window with remarkable varieties of the pleasures of life, remarkable life.' As Louis Aragon puts it in 'Mimosas', in this poem Al-Saddiq extends his hand to the subway and they both emerge from the ground to breathe.

In 2021 I attempted to puzzle out the strange phrases, allusions and metaphors in 'The Book of Sorrows' in order to create a film based on the poem. Al-Saddiq was very excited to hear about the film and to consider new ways to experiment with poetry. He is always open to exploring the vast possibilities of poetry and poetry translation that other forms of media empower.

I had planned to spend three days with Al-Saddiq to shoot the film. I was in a hurry. In the very early hours of our meeting, I asked Al-Saddiq, 'What is the "remarkable life"?'

Al-Saddiq didn't answer me with words.

We started our journey from Queensway, a busy thoroughfare in west London. We grabbed some falafel sandwiches and sat to eat in Hyde Park while talking about modern Iraqi poetry. Al-Saddiq gave me a tour of each of his haunts in those early years, including a tiny makeshift nest on the second floor, a little falafel shop, his local pub, and several bookstores, as well as the corner where the Sudanese gather to play dominoes while they run their businesses.

Then, in the same way Sufis commemorate the death of their forebears, we visited the house of Sarah Maguire, founder of the Poetry Translation Centre and a champion of Al-Saddiq's work in translation, to keep her legacy and memory alive.

*

Al-Saddiq once told me that he is inspired by the Sudanese poet Muhammad Mahdi al-Majzob, quoting him: 'I dream of a generation that makes writing as essential a part of living as drinking water'. For Al-Saddiq, to write is to live. His poetry is an attempt to establish our interconnectedness and foster a sense of community. Like a dervish, Al-Saddiq is seeking comfort and emotional relief in times of trauma and grief. Poetry, and this translation project, is an attempt to understand the 'strangeness of the sounds' and climb over the 'wall of language'. It is looking for familiarity in a place where: 'Everything… / Everything… / Invokes your exile / Everything shouts: *Hey, lonely!*'

Every time Al-Saddiq and I meet, every time we read, translate, and live out a poem, every time we cry and laugh to our bones, every time we gossip about the poets who couldn't keep up the good work – that is the remarkable life.

Bryar Bajalan, Exeter, 2023

Poems

ما اسمكِ؟!

أتعلّمُ أبجد كونكِ، كلّ ثانية أتّقيكِ فيها
أتعلّمكِ على الهوى مباشرةً
فمُك مسجدُ الفَم المُشتهى
ولحنوّكِ راياتٍ لا حصرَ لها

*

ليس اسْمُكِ اسمٌ ولا وصفَ لَك
أنتِ... أنتِ
ولا حرفَ يصلُحُ
يصلحُ رُمْحُكِ فرساً تُعْجِزُ زوبعة الريح
روحُكِ تُعْجِزُ جوهرة الرُّوح

*

أتعلّمُ اسْمَكِ ووَسْمَكِ
أتعلّمُ حتّى ألاقيك!

What Is Your Name?!

Every second of my worship I'm learning the alphabet of you
I'm learning you from love itself
Your mouth is a mosque for my lustful tongue
Your love welcomes me with countless flags…

*

Your name does not name or describe you
You are you
No letters can contain you
Your gait is a gallop, you outrun the whirlwind
Your soul outruns the essence of a soul

*

I am learning your name and your being
I am learning you, until we meet again!

مطبخ الصديقة

جدارُ اللّغةِ لم يكُ فاصلاً في مطبخ الصديقةْ
في مطبخ الصديقةِ موقدُ الجسـم أشعَلَهُ اللّيْلُ
كأسُ الشايِّ وإبريق النبيذ
التعاطفُ الفذُّ مع طفولةِ العاطفةْ
المكانُ الغريبُ
الاسمُ الغريبُ
الضحكةُ المستثارةُ من غربةِ الصّوتِ
والشمعة على حافة "البانيو" تستعطفُ ألسنةَ الوَجْدِ والرائحةْ

*

ثمة أيقونةٌ نادرةَ النّحَتِ قُربَ العُنقْ
ثمة العنق...
ثمة الإبط، والسُرّة...
ثمة ما تعتنق الرّوحَ – بلا ترجمانْ

*

جدارُ اللّغةِ...
والكلماتِ العاطلةِ
ليلتها...
ثمَّ مجمرةُ الوَصْلِ والأدعيةْ!

A Friend's Kitchen

The wall of language was no barrier, in a friend's kitchen
In a friend's kitchen, night lit up the body's stove
Teacup and wine jug
Her toddling love, uniquely hers
A strange place
A strange name
And laughter, provoked by the strangeness of the sounds
And the candle on the bathtub's edge, its beckoning
    tongue and my beloved's scent

*

Such a holy symbol, hidden in the nape of her neck!
Such a neck!
Such an armpit, such a navel!
And my soul's submission, no translation needed

*

The wall of language
And that night's
Worthless words
And then the censer of arrival and the prayers

أنثى

١

كأسُ البُنِّ عذراءُ تطلبُ رأسَك
مغناجةً تتلوى على النارِ
تُنْضِجُ روحَكِ في الرائحةِ
تتشهّاكَ كاملةَ العُريِّ
قبل أنْ تَنْضجَ تُصبحُ كأسَك!

٢

هذي الليلة لك
سيّدة اللّيل والظهيرة، سيّدة البُنِّ والشجنِ الطقسيِّ
ليلتُك الملكيّة، حَفيّةٌ بأنْسَكِ الـمَكيِّ
بسيرةِ الحمامةِ، بسورةِ العنكبوتْ!

٣

الثانية عشر ليلاً...
فمُكِ يلعبُ بالحجَرِ والنارِ
ألتذُّ بالعنصر الخامس في طَبْخةِ الرّيح والماء
الثانية صباحاً
لسانُ شارعٍ يشربُ مِنْ فَمِ الهاويةْ

Female

1

A pristine cup of coffee begs for your brain
Flirting, rippling across the fire
It ripens your soul with its scent
It lusts for you, entirely naked
Before it is brewed, it becomes yours!

2

This night is for you
Lady of my night and noon, lady of coffee and sorrow
Your queenly night of Meccan celebration
By the story of the dove, the surah of the spider!

3

Twelve at night…
Your mouth plays with stone and fire
Mine savours the fifth element
I rouse by heating wind and water
Two in the morning
A tongue emerges to sip from the mouth of the abyss

أفتقدك!

١

أدركتني الحياةُ – عِلَّةٌ لا شفاءَ منها
حتى أنني أموتُ كلَّ ثانيةٍ أتنفَّس فيها!

٢

أدبِّرُ أمري – على كلّ حالٍ
مُغبِّراً كلَّ غروبٍ
في الدروب التي بين قبرك وقبري!

٣

دمعتي ماعونُها دفءُ صدْرِكِ
يدي تنبضُ بيدكِ
كأسي أوحشَتها اللّيالي!

I Miss You

1

Life overtook me – an illness with no remedy
I am dying with each passing breath!

2

I take care of my business, anyway
Dusty each dusk
Along the path between your grave and mine

3

The bowl of my tears is the warmth in your chest
My hand pulses with yours
The nights desolate my cup!

Panic Attack

نعم، سننفقُ على هذه اللعبةِ الخطرة، من حسابنا السرِّي، يوم القيامةْ
ليس معقولاً أبداً، أن أنسى بهذه الطريقة

طعمَ ضحكةٍ مطهوَّةٍ بغنجٍ جيّدٍ، لأردَّ على رسالةٍ في الهاتف
أو أن أتجاهل هاتف اللحظة المبهّرة، بلا حساب!

*

ظلّت النافذةُ مغلقةً نحو ٤ أسابيع
لكن صوتَ القطارات لا يزالُ نافذاً، منذ الخامسة صباحاً
لن تذهب ثأراتي سُدىً
صدِّقيني
ستحصلين على حصتِكِ ممّا حصل!

*

السرابُ ليس كلُه سراباً!

Panic Attack

Yes, on Resurrection Day we will pay from our secret account
How could I think only of myself? Impossible

The taste of a laugh simmered with flirtation, answering a
　　letter on the phone
Ignoring the breathtaking moment of a call's ring, paying it
　　no account!

*

The window remained closed for nearly four weeks
But the sound of trains still carried through, from five in the
　　morning
My revenge will not be in vain
Believe me
You will get your due!

*

A mirage is not all mirage

Tattoo

ليس بالضرورةِ قُرْبَ غابةٍ صغيرةٍ أو حديقةٍ
تهاتِفُكَ في ظهيرةِ صيفٍ ما
ربما: تهاتفُك الواحدة صباحاً
تَشْهَقُ لمجرى الجُرحِ، لأثرِ مَرأى الجُرح في الشريانِ
لأثرِ مَرأى الجُرح القديمْ!

كلُّ شيء كان مُعدًّا بعنايةٍ فائقة
لذلك حلَّقت الفراشات مُلوّنة – ساعة الله المُتْقنة
بَرَقَ كلُّ شيءٍ
وهي تُسبِّحُ بحمد الذي لا يُعدُّ ولا يُقاس

قلتُ لكِ ما لم أقلْ
شهقتُكِ قالتْ كلَّ شيء
يَدُكِ على يدي، كوب الشايْ وكأس القهوةِ الحنونْ
ليس أكثرَ من قُبْلتكِ قبل أن أقولَ وداعاً

أتقنتُ أن أحفظ سرَّكِ
أتقنتُ نسيانكِ، لكنما مهرجانُ الذي بين فخذيك
لكنما مهرجان الفراشاتِ والأخضرِ الكوكبيْ
عند ظَهركِ المُشتهى
المهرجانُ – المهرجان!

ثوبُ ذئبةٍ آخر اللَّيلِ يبرُزُ
يبرزُ ثوب الحنانْ!

Tattoo

Not necessarily near a little forest or garden
Your calls on a summer afternoon
Perhaps: your calls at one in the morning
Climb toward the source of the wound
Climb the wound's path till the trail reveals
The artery's festering wound!

Everything was carefully prepared
So the butterflies flew, scattering colour – God's perfect hour
Everything lightened
And she exalted the uncountable, unmeasurable one

I told you what I did not say
Your inhale has said it all
Your hand on my hand, a glass of tea and a cup of coffee less warm
Than your kiss at my goodbye

I mastered keeping your secret
I mastered forgetting you, except for the festival between your thighs
Except for the festival of butterflies and planetary green
On your coveted back
The festival – the festival!

At night's end, the wolf's dress appears, rises
A dress of tenderness emerges!

... وأنتِ لا تعودني

مريضٌ يشرفُ عليه أطباء وممرضون لا مرئيين، العربةُ ترقصُ خضمَ الليل من جسرٍ إلى آخر نافذةٍ تعبرُها العَينُ، فلا تنبّهُ حديقةٌ عناقَ ثعالبها العشاق؛ كدت ألمسُ وجهَكِ ليلتها: أشرفتُ على الغرق في كيمياء المحاليلِ الوريدية - مرّةً، بدا بستانُكِ عالياً، بدوتُ محلّقاً نحو قعرِ الهاويةِ، لم تكُ تلكَ - بالطبع - مأثرتي!

And You Don't Return to Me

A patient, supervised by invisible doctors and nurses. The ambulance dances in the middle of the night, from a bridge to the last window the eye can span; the garden does not break the embrace of its loving foxes; I almost touched your face that night. I almost sank into the chemistry of your IV fluids. Your orchard seemed so high up, and I seemed to fly to the bottom of the abyss, but that was not – of course – my miracle!

كتابُ المراثي

في عتمةِ الغرفةِ الصغيرة قربَ محطةِ القطاراتِ الكبيرة؛ كان الشتاءُ الأوَّلُ؛ شغيلةٌ آخرَ اللّيلِ صخبُهم لوَّنَ النافذةَ الوحيدة بأصنافَ نادرةٍ من بهجةِ الحياة - الحياةَ النادرةُ.

صوتُكِ الساخن على الهاتف ألهبَ ظَهْرَ الشتاءِ بسوطِ الغنج الحريفِ بينما يتهافتُ المطرُ خلف زجاجِ سيارةٍ تنهبُ الجسرَ نحو الهاويةِ.

ليست محطةُ القطاراتِ وحدها؛ ليس خطَّ الهاتف الساخنِ أو ما تكنزُ نافذةٌ صغيرةٌ في إطارِ الشاشةِ من صبوات، ليس اسْمُكِ أو رقمَ الغرفةِ لا لونَ النافذةُ.

نسجُ الأصابعِ وحده كان مُلِهِمًّا؛ رقم سيارةِ الإسعافِ وألوان الصندوق!

The Book of Sorrows

It was my first winter in the darkness of the small room near the big train station; the bustling of late-night workers coloured my lonely window with remarkable varieties of the pleasures of life, remarkable life.

Your warm voice on the phone ignited winter's spine with a flaming, flirtatious whip, while the rain splattered against the window of a car moving so fast it seemed to drag the bridge towards the abyss.

Not just the train station, not your warm voice on the line, not the nostalgia hoarded in the tiny window of my screen, not your name or room number, not the colours in the window.

Our interwoven fingers stirred something in their own right, as did the number for the ambulance, the many colours of the box!

121

١

بين كأسِ الـ "هوت شوكلت" الذي طَلَبْتُهُ، أولَ مَرَّةٍ
وسخونة الهاتف على الخدِّ في الطرف الآخر، كلَّ ليلةٍ
رقمٌ واحدٌ
تأويلُهُ لا يفسِّرُ حَمَّاماً ساخِناً
أو عَرَقاً أغرقَ ليلتَها بالفرح المُعافى
كشفَ سِحْرَ التّفاحةِ اللّعوبْ

٢

رقم الهاتفِ الذي لا يردُّ
البصُّ الذي لن يصلَ قبل ٢٧ دقيقة
الصبيّةُ الغريبةُ التي تجهش بالبكاء، قربَكَ
في الخامسةِ من صباح الأحدْ
ولا تجرؤُ على أن تطيِّبَ خاطرها
قنينة الـ فودكا المهشَّمة على الرصيف
كلُّ شيءٍ
كلُّ شيءٍ
يناديك بالغربة
كلُّ شيءٍ يهتفُ بكَ: يا وحيدْ!

121

1

Between the first cup of hot chocolate I ever ordered
And the heat of the phone against my cheek on the other end,
   every night
One number
Dialling it does not justify a hot bath
Or this sweat drowning the night with its healthy joy
Nor does it uncover the magic of that flirtatious apple

2

The phone number that no one answers
The bus that won't arrive for another 27 minutes
The strange girl, sobbing beside you
At five o'clock on a Sunday morning
You dare not even comfort her
The bottle of vodka
Smashed on the pavement
Everything…
Everything…
Invokes your exile
Everything shouts: *Hey, lonely!*

٣

لأكتبَ لكِ أو عنكِ ينبغي أن أتَّبعَ مجرى الجدولِ الصغيرْ
لابدّ أن أُحسنَ الإصغاءَ لخطوي يلهثُ إثر خطوكِ
دون أن أبلغَ مسافةَ حرفِكِ أو أولَ درجاتِ السلّمْ

الفصولُ كانت هناك:
دفعةً واحدةً، لأولَ مرّةٍ
تنبضُ بأجنحةِ الملائكةِ الآبقينْ.
ثمة كوكبٌ اسْمُه لم يُولَدْ بعدْ.
ثمة إلهٍ يتخلّقُ توًّا من سِحْرِ المخلوقْ.

لا يصلحُ لمنادمتي أحدٌ
غيرُ منقوصٍ ينادمُ غيرَ منقوصٍ
ثلّةٌ تخلعُ حُلّةٌ.

بينما تركض عربةُ ليلٍ إثرَ ليلٍ بلا عربة
أتنادى مهيضَ الجناحِ لنبعٍ يحنُّ
على مسجدِ الدرويش تتنادى لياليكِ منقوشةً
إبريقُهُ يَبْرِقُ بلا حاجةٍ لكمالِ العروشْ.

3

To write to or about you, I must follow the streambed
I must listen carefully for breathless footfall so I can trace your steps
Without reaching your borders or the topmost stair

Where I find every season
All at once, for the first time
They pulse on the wings of dark angels
There is a nameless, peerless planet yet to be born
There is a God, born now from the magic of the created

No one is worthy of my companionship
Some forebears strip off their vestments
Only the spotless may accompany the spotless

While night's wheel pursues a wheelless night
Broken-winged, I call on a compassionate spring
Your nights, engraved on the dervish's mosque, call to me
His ritual pitcher gleams with no need for the splendour of a throne

فئةٌ باغيةْ

محضُ كنّاسٍ وصانعُ أحذيةْ
كنتُ أتجوَّلُ في ساحةِ الاعتصامْ
لا أصلحُ ان أكون شهيداً
هل أصلحُ ان أكون شاهداً؟!
بينما يشهد النيلُ على جثتي؟!

*

هناك في غرفة نائية
يكونُ غيابي عن الآلِ والأهلِ
عن حضنِ الحبيبةِ
في ضاحيةٍ نائية
عن المدينة وبهرجها الطاغيةْ

*

هناك
ربما
يشهد الطاغيةْ
تشهد الفئة الباغيةْ!

The Aggressors

Just an ordinary streetsweeper and cobbler
I was walking by the protest on the public square
I'm not fit to be a martyr
Am I fit to be a witness?!
While the Nile witnesses my corpse?!

*

There, in a room on the outskirts
My absence from among my kith and kin
From my beloved's lap
In a suburb on the outskirts
Of the city with its immoral tyrant

*

There
Perhaps
The tyrant witnesses it
The aggressors witness it!

أوراق اللجوءْ

١

خمسة وعشرون عاماً أَنْفَقْتُها نقدًا في حانة المنفى
أدرسُ جمجمةَ الوقتِ على طاولةٍ صدئة
هتف لي عنصر الساكسفون من حنجرةِ الأبديةْ
من ندمٍ أَسْبَقُ
هتفت بي خسارةُ اليومْ

ما المنفى؟!

٢

السابقُ بيتُ الطِّينِ، رائحةُ التَّبغِ تأذنُ للصباح أن يطلَّ
كوبُ الشايِّ، لغو الجيرانِ والصحيفة
نَصْبُ الأملِ على ساريةِ العَزْم
نسيانُ مجزرةَ الأَمْسِ
طهو المسافاتِ أو تَوُّقع يوم جديدْ

*

النِّظامُ أتلفَ يومَكَ
رأسُمالِكَ وقتٌ على مقلبِ النفايات

٣

الكأسُ الخامسةُ أو الخامسةُ صباحاً
في غرفةِ الفندقِ

Asylum Papers

1

I spent twenty-five years in exile's bar, all in cash
Examining time's skull on a rusty table
The saxophone screeched at me from eternity's throat
From an old regret I've challenged to a race
For screeching my wasted day:

What is exile?!

2

In the past:
A house of mud – the smell of tobacco permitting the
    morning to rise –
A cup of tea, the neighbours's chatter and the newspaper
Raising hope on the mast of determination
Forgetting yesterday's massacre
Simmering our separation or anticipating a new day.

*

Bureaucracy ruined your day
Your capital is time in the landfill

3

A fifth drink or five in the morning
My companion in the hotel room

ثمة مَنْ تشربُ الوقتَ
لا تَعْبُرُ الكأسَ حاسرةَ الرأسِ
أو تَعْبُرُ القُبْلَةَ فارغةَ الكأسِ
بيني وبين السجارة ثمة ما يخطرُ على البال
بينها وغطاء السرير ما لا يخطرُ على البال
بيدَ أن الصباحَ يُطلُّ
بين الإشارةِ واسمها
أو بين الوسائدِ والقطن
تمرقُ الشمسُ ولا يغربُ الأمسُ

٤

المنفى جَوَّافَةٌ أتذكرُ نشوتَها حين أسكنُ
أو حين لا يسكنُ إلاّ مذاق التذكّرِ
أذكر أسماء من غادروا واحداً - واحدةً
كنتُ واحدهمْ
أذكر أسماء من قُبِروا
أذكرُ اسمكِ أو اسم من يُولدُ
كان منفى
ولياليكِ بلا حسابٍ

٥

تحتاجُ إلى جِذْرٍ لتَسْكُنَ التُّرْبَةَ
معرفةٌ باطنيةٌ بأُمِّ الحَجَرِ وفصائلِ النّباتِ
بخصائصِ الفصولِ وأنواع الزّواحفِ
بشعوبِ الطّيرِ... إلخ.

تحتاجُ الكثيرَ لتكونَ غَيرَك!

Devours time
You don't grasp for the cup but bow your head in respect
Nor do you grasp for a kiss with an empty cup
Between me and the cigarette something comes to mind
Between the cigarette and the bedcover something that
    wouldn't occur to you
But the morning emerges
Between the sign and its name
Or between the pillows and their cotton
The sun goes down but yesterday has yet to set

4

Exile is a void – I remember its ecstasy when I make my home
Or when the only thing to make its home is the taste of
    remembrance
I remember the names of those who departed, one by one
I was one of them
I remember the names of those who were buried
I remember your name or the names of those yet to be born
This was exile
With its countless nights

5

You need roots to establish yourself in the soil
Esoteric knowledge of petrology and the taxonomy of plants
Reptilian species and the nature of the seasons
The phyla of birds, etc.

You need so much to be someone else

Queensway

١

يومٌ عُمُرُهُ سِتٌ وثلاثون ساعةً، يوم أوراقنا تضرّجتْ بِدَم المَرَحْ، ظلّي وظلّكِ جِسْمٌ واحدٌ، تُجهِشُ منهُ الفواكهُ، يوم شربنا عمرنا كلّه دفعةً واحدةً؛ صوتُكِ أيقظَ صورتكِ المُطفأة - ظلّتْ مُضاءةً خمسة عشر عاماً - بقاربٍ نائم عند مقرن النيلين؛ نظارةُ الشمس وقمحِ الضحكة اللّعوبِ في ردهة مطعم الـ أنجيرا القَارِه، بلذعة الجنزبيل وسلطنة الممكنات.

الصّيفُ كان ضيفاً هناك، في الحانة ليس ثمة من يكترث، فمُكِ الخاطئُ في المكان الصحيح، في لعثمة الطريق أومض الفندق: هناك ما يكفي من التبغ والنبيذ، ما يكفي لفضح الليل والتستُّر على الكَمَاْل.

٢

مطرٌ خفيفٌ أيقظَ الصباحَ - هذا الصباح: لم أكُ نائماً؛ أعرفُ الطريق إلى المطار وأحفظ عن ظهر قلبٍ رقمَ الرحلة وموعد الوصول واسم شركة الطيران، الشموعُ التي غادرتِها الأسبوع الماضي ناعسةٌ، لا تزال ناعسةً، المطبخُ على حاله والحمّامُ في مكانه - يا للدهشة؛ هذا الصباح اخترته من بين صباحاتٍ عديدةٍ قدمها لي الشبّاك!

Queensway

1

A day that was thirty-six hours old, a day our leaves were streaked with joy's blood – my shadow and yours forming one body, whose fruits ripen and ripen – the day we drained our whole life in a single shot. Your voice awakened your extinguished image – it has remained lit for fifteen years – with a boat sleeping where the two Niles meet. Your sunglasses and your sparkling laugh in the grand lobby of the Anjera – a spike of wheat, pungent ginger, the sultanate of possibilities.

Summer was a guest there. In the pub nobody cared about your wrong mouth in the right place. In the stuttering of the road, the hotel glowed: there was enough tobacco and wine, enough to expose the night and cover up perfection.

2

This morning, a light rain woke the morning: I was not asleep. I know the road to the airport by heart, the flight number, its time of arrival and the airline's name, the drowsy candles you left last week are just as drowsy still, the kitchen hasn't changed, the bathroom in its place – wonderment: I chose this morning from among the many offered to me by my window!

٣

صورتي صوتك المشوَّش أو صيرورتي جِذْرُ تَبَدُّدٍ تَخْشِيتَهُ

تلك أيقونةُ الفَقْدِ والوَجْدِ؟!

الليلةَ الماضيةَ صوتُكِ على الموبايلِ أَثْمَلَ المارةَ حين كنتُ أَعبُرُ الشَارعَ، كان الجميعُ في حالةِ رقصٍ فادحٍ، ليس قُرب حانةٍ أو أيِّ شيءٍ، ذلك في الطريقِ القصيرِ من مكتبةِ الساقي حتى التقاطُعِ الأوَّلِ الذي أتَّخذه صعوداً نحو الـ هايد بارك، نحو عشَّنا المؤقت الصَّغير في الطابق الثاني - يَرقُبُ مَقْدِمكِ، يتشوَّقُ للَّمْسَةِ الحانيةُ ونبضكِ الحريفْ!

٤

أُبُهةٌ شخصيةٌ لأجلها يَبرقُ تاجُكَ، حين تطلبُ سيجارةً من عَابرٍ آخرَ اللَّيلِ ولا يستجيبُ بتكبُّرٍ مُتحضِّرٍ، ليستْ مسألةَ نقودٍ، آخرَ الليلِ هنا شخوصه شخوصُ آخرِ اللَّيلِ، تحضُّرٌ متفهِّمٌ لكوكبِ شخصٍ غيرُ آبهٍ لكوكب شخصٍ آخرْ.

نَقَدْتُكَ آخرَ قَطْرَةٍ من الجسم قبلها
آبهاً لدوائرَ الجَذْبِ - أولُ عابرٍ
سطوتُه تَكْمُنُ بلا صولجانٍ
بطفولةٍ عُمُرُهَا مائةَ عامٍ مُقْبِلٍ
تقطفُ جوهرَها في كَسْرٍ من ثانيةٍ - أومضتْ - مَضَتْ!

3

My image, your distorted voice, and my impermanence: the roots of the separation you fear.

Vessels of annihilation and bliss?!

Last night your voice on my mobile phone intoxicated the pedestrians passing by as I crossed the street. Everyone seemed to dance wildly, with not a pub in sight, on the short distance from the Al Saqi Bookstore to my first turn toward Hyde Park, towards our tiny, makeshift nest on the second floor – its eyes on your feet, longing for your intoxicating touch and your exquisite pulse!

4

Your crown gleams with splendour when you ask for a cigarette from a passerby at the end of the night and he, with civilised arrogance, does not reply. It's not a matter of money – here the late night has its characters, its late-night characters, a civilisation built on the understanding that each spinning world cares not to understand any other.

I pay you upfront, the last drop of my body
Noting the charge of attraction between us
    I rob him – the first passerby – an authority with no sceptre
        With a childhood of a hundred years to come
           Intuiting its essence in a fraction of a second –
           Flashing – fleeting!

*

هنا أو هناك
كلُّ ليلةٍ - آخرَ الليلِ - أقترحُ نخبَ موتي وأنجو...

٥

لٰكن مُخْلصاً أنساكِ أول ناصيةٍ لا أراكِ فيها
أنسى اسمكِ واسمي
خصائصَ أوهامي
رموزَ حضوركِ في الحلم
أبجدَ مذهبكِ الباطنيُّ - ترجمانُه بجسمي وجسمكِ
لٰكن مُخْلصاً
لا أثمر سُبَّةَ التماثلِ

*

يشبهني أن أنسلَّ وحيداً بلا مثالٍ أو أيَّ شيءٍ!

*

Here or there
Every night – late, at its very end – I toast my death and survive…

5

To be frank, I will forget you as soon as I round the first corner
Forget your name and my own
    The character of my illusions
    The symbols of your presence in my dreams
    The alphabet of your esoteric doctrine – its interpretation,
        in my body and yours
To be frank
With me the curse of sameness bears no fruit

*

It's so like me to slip away, alone!

تلك تيجانهم

حديقةُ الله أبوابُها مفتوحةٌ للعصافيرِ
بستانُه أرحبُ
تلك تيجانهم مضرجةٌ بأمانيّهمْ

*

تلك أرواحُهم تطرقُ أبوابكَ طرقاً طفيفاً
لها عبقُ توقٍ لفجرٍ يضيءُ باسمكَ
عدلاً وحريةً وسلاماً
بأرضٍ بَسطتَها باسمكَ لهمْ
ولأسلافِهم ونسلِهمْ
مفاتيحُها اسمكَ واسمكُ الخَاتمُ - جلَّ عُلاه

*

عند بابهِ
يكشفُ الدَمَ عمَّا به
يطلعُ طلحُ أرواحِ الصبايا - العَبَقْ
والصبيةُ أرواحُهم تَأتلقْ
في أتونِ النزالِ النَزِقْ
الصدورُ مكشوفةٌ للرصاص
لا شيءَ غير الخلاصْ
عند بابهْ
يطلع الدم متقدًّا في إهابهْ

*

أخجلُ أن أكتب حرفاً
الدمُ - بعدُ - لم يَجَفّ
يخجلُ الحَرفُ!

Their Crowns

God's Garden welcomes the birds
His orchard is vast
They tarnished their crowns with desire

*

Those are their souls knocking softly at Your many doors
Their fragrance longs for a dawn to break in Your name
Justice, freedom and peace
In a land spread out in Your name
And for their ancestors and their descendants
Its keys are Your name and Your name is the ultimate – *Jalah 'alāhu!*

*

At Your doorstep
The blood reveals its story
The lauded souls of young women emerge
And the souls of boys flare
In the furnace of a reckless battle
Chests are exposed to bullets
 Nothing but salvation
At Your doorstep
The blood comes out of hiding

*

I am ashamed to write a single letter
The blood has not yet dried –
The letter is ashamed!

Homeless

وجاء وقتٌ ليس في وسعِهِ أن يتناسلَ
جاء وقتٌ لا يَسعُ الذكرى
جاء وقتٌ بلا حاجةٍ
جاء وقتٌ بلا حاجةٍ للوقتْ!

*

وقلتُ لك إن الحكايا لا تفي المُجْمَل
لن يثمرَ الجدارُ سوى ظلٍّ يتيمْ
يُتْمٌ تأكلُهُ الحَاجَةُ لحفنةِ شمسٍ عابرةُ

*

ثم هناك السلّمِ المكسورِ في العتبةِ الخامسةُ

بقايا ماءٍ راكدٍ في البئرِ
كراسةٌ طُمِسَتْ سطورُها
إثرَ وطءِ النّعالِ العسكري على الوجه
وهناك دماءٌ

Homeless

There came a time with no strength to reproduce
A time with no room for remembrance
A time with no use
A time with no need for time!

*

I've told you that the stories don't add up
The wall will bear nothing but an orphan shadow
Worn down by its need for a handful of a fleeting sunlight

*

And then there is the broken ladder at the fifth threshold

Traces of stagnant water in the well
A notebook, its lines trampled
By the tread of military boots on its face
And there is blood

كدت أنساك

الحربُ انتهتْ يوم الأربعاءْ
يوم الاثنين كانت السماءُ صافيةً
الأرضُ لم تعد لعبةً
في يد من يصبغونَها بدمِ ابن آدمْ

*

تذكرتُ وقعَ أقدامها قرب بابي
قبل خمسين قرنٍ من الرياحينِ
والشوقُ دافقٌ
هل تذكرتُ طيفَ العناقْ؟!

*

كانت الشجرةْ
كانت البئرُ
كان حبلٌ مُدلًّى على حافةِ السِرِّ
كانت البذرةُ حُبْلَى
والحُلّةُ درويشُهَا عارياً
!في لباسِ الحنينْ!

Nearly Forgot You

The war ended on Wednesday
On Monday the sky was clear
Earth is no longer a game
To those who dye it red with the blood of Adam's sons

*

I remember her footsteps outside my door
Fifty years before basil
And my longing gushes up
Do you remember some trace of our embrace?

*

There was a tree
There was a well
There was a rope dangling from the secret's edge
The seed was pregnant
The tunic, its dervish was naked
Beneath the tunic of longing!

جثتي في النهر

القتلةُ يرقصونَ على جثتي
كنت أحظى بما يكفي من الفرح
قبل الرصاصةِ الغادرةْ!
كانت الساحةُ مكتظةً بالحلمِ والأملْ
أظنُّها لا تزال وهي تحدِّثُ عن دمي
لا يزالُ الحلمُ والأملْ
في ميدانِ الاعتصام مُلهمًا
الصبايا والفتياتِ - الأمهاتِ والزغاريدْ
صُنع الطعام؛ والصبية وهمّة الشباب
كلُّ شيءٍ يثيرُ شهيةَ الحياةْ
الأغنياتْ
الرسوم البهيجة؛ والتعاويذ؛ والدعواتْ
كنتُ أبهى وانا أتجوَّلُ في ساحةِ المهرجانْ
أزهو - وهو ترابي
أزهو - وهو وطني
وانا كلمةُ السرِّ نحوها ونحوه
انا سيّدُ المكان والإمكانْ!
لا تزالُ جُثّتي على النَهر
أنصتُ عميقاً لطرْقِ الرفاق على النفَقْ
وعلى جسرِ الحديدِ - كيفما اتفقْ
أصغي لهديلِ الحماماتِ
ذواتِ العبَقْ - وزغاريدهنَّ أبهى ما يكونُ الألقْ
لا زلتُ أنتقي الأُنْسَ وأنا موغلٌ في الغرقْ!

جُثَّتي على النَهر - لا تزالْ
ولا زلتُ منصتاً وبهيجاً بصوتِ الرفيقاتِ - الرفاقْ
لازلتُ مبتهجاً بالعناقْ

My Corpse in the River

The killers are dancing on my body
I had joy enough
Before the traitorous bullet
The square was full of hopes and dreams
I think it still is, now spurred by my blood
On the protest square
Hopes and dreams
Still glimmer
Women of all ages – the mothers and their ululations
Making food
And the young men with their youthful zeal
Everything stimulates our will to live!
The songs
The cheerful graffiti, the incantations and prayers
I become magnificent exploring the festive square
I'm blooming – this is my soil
I'm blooming – this is my homeland
And I am the link between them
I am the master of this place and possibility!
My body is still in the river
I listen carefully to my comrades' banging on the tunnel
And on the iron bridge – just as we had agreed
I listen to the doves' cooing
So fragrant – and their trilling, brighter than brightness
I still choose joy and I'm close to drowning!

My body is in the river – still
And I listen still, delighted by the voices of my comrades

نسيتُ هديرَ الرصاصِ الهطيلِ وغدرِ الجُنَاةْ
لازلتُ أصغي لزغرودةٍ - فيصلّ بين الحياةِ وبين المماتْ
أعيشُ على خيطِ عطرٍ طفيفٍ
لا أزالُ أعيشُ وجُثتي على النّهر
تعيشُ الحياةُ!

Still delighted by their embraces
I forget the roaring torrent of bullets and betrayals
I am still listening to the ululations – till the very end
I survive by the thinnest thread of a scent
Still alive, my body in the river
Living this life!

سأموتُ يوم الأربعاء!

الطيورُ التي أبهجتْ صدركِ
الصباحُ الذي تنتقيه كلَّ صباحٍ من النافذة
اشتباكُ المرايا وألوان "البلوزةِ"
مع الصباح الذي يشتهيكِ!

الحديقةُ التي لم نتعانق فيها
القبلةُ الكوكبية في سلّم البناية المظلم
فَمُكِ
فَمُكِ الفَذّ
فستانُكِ الذي لا يكترثُ!

أرهقني صمتُكِ الجارح
أرهقتني مراياكِ
اشتباكُ الحديقةِ ودرج السلّم المكسور
أرهقني أن أناديكِ
طرف الإصبع المحترقِ بالحِنّاء!

أرهقتني القصيدةُ التي لن تكتملْ!

I Will Die on Wednesday!

The birds that cheered you up
The morning you hand-pick each morning from your window
The colours of that blouse tangling in the mirror
With the morning you crave!

The garden where we didn't hug
The planetary kiss in the building's dark staircase
Your mouth
What a mouth
Your reckless dress!

Your painful silence exhausted me
Your mirrors exhausted me
The tangling of the garden and the overgrown staircase
It exhausted me to call you
Your fingertip charred with henna exhausted me!

I am exhausted by the poem I will never complete!

لا أحد!

في زحامِ معسكرِ اللاجئينْ
الصبايا الوحيداتِ
يَتهنَّ، الصبايا اللواتي فُقِدْنَ – ذاتَ ليلٍ
وما مِن أثرْ!

من يدلُّ الملاكَ؟!
من يدلُّ الغزالةَ للنبعِ؟!
هل مِنْ مُدَّكِرْ؟!

كانت الطريقُ إلى البئرِ والحقلِ
هي الطريقُ إلى البئرِ والحقلِ
الطريقُ إلى ساحةِ الرقصِ والأسبازْ
لم تكُ الظلمةُ والسكّينُ تبرقُ غدّارةً
والوحوشْ

في زحامِ المعسكرِ
من يتفقدُ نبضَ الوحيداتْ؟!

No One!

In the crowded refugee camp
The lonely girls
Are missing, kidnapped one night
Without a trace!

Who guides the angel?!
Who guides the deer to the spring?!
Is there anyone who will be mindful?!

The way to the well and the field was
Just the way to the well and the field
The way to the dance and the rituals
It wasn't darkness and the glint of a knife
It wasn't full of monsters

In the crowded camp
Who checks the lonely girls' pulse?!

من كتاب المحو

السُرَّةُ مدفونةٌ قرب غرفةٍ طينيةٍ
قبل خمسة عقودٍ، في "ابوروف"
السيرةُ مدفونةٌ في السريرةُ!

*

ليس سِرّاً: أن تعبثَ بِكَ الحياةُ
ليس سِرّاً: أن تعبثَ بالحياةِ!

*

لن أسردَ أيّ شيءٍ
أنا مشغولٌ بكنسِ أثري في الوجودْ
لن يتبقَّى أيّ شيءْ!

From the Book of Erasure

The umbilical cord is buried near a mud room
Five decades ago, in Aburov
My biography buried in the bed!

*

It's no secret: life messes you up
It's no secret: you're messing with life!

*

I will narrate nothing
I am busy sweeping away all traces of my existence
Nothing will be left!

Afterword

By the time he had turned 40 in 2010, Al-Saddiq Al-Raddi had published a *Collected Poems*, gathering work from three earlier collections that had established his reputation as a new and formidable presence in modern Sudanese and Arabic poetry. He had also gained respect as an important and fearless journalist in Khartoum, the city of his birth. The work in his *Collected Poems* is in part presented in English in *A Monkey At The Window: Selected Poems* (Poetry Translation Centre/Bloodaxe Books, 2016). Yet just two years later, in 2012, he was living a very different life, a life in exile in London. It is the experiences of exile – the life that exile forces on those who are exiled, but also, and no less, the knowledge of the struggles of those still back 'home', and with all the questions as to the frail valencies of 'home' – that the poetry of *A Friend's Kitchen* addresses.

There is a short poem quite early in the book, 'I Miss You', which particularly struck me. It is just eight lines long, though divided into three sections (2/3/3) it seems longer, stretched beyond its measure, increasing both itself and our understanding by its silences. Silences are not easy to measure, but this poem gifts us its silences. Consider the opening stanza:

> Life overtook me – an illness with no remedy
> I am dying with each passing breath!

Its fifteen words in English are a sort of essence of the whole collection, throughout which other silences constantly resound. Such silences are not negating, rather they are part of the poet's Sufi sensibility. Islamic and Quranic references are woven throughout the poet's language, both explicitly and by association, and their presence more often than not evokes an Islam of tenderness and the poet's earlier life in Sudan, in an Arabic of Africa, acting at times as sounding boards, as memory vessels for the currency of new experience. Thus lines such as 'Vessels of annihilation and bliss' or 'A mirage is not all mirage'.

The word 'abyss' occurs three times in the first poems of the book, as if to fix our minds and spirits on fracture and ruptured lives (translator Bryar Bajalan meditates well on this in his introduction). Al-Raddi's Sufisms are almost strongest when he invokes the body in his poems, as if try to stay the abyss, or to stave off unavoidable failure, or to hold pain in abeyance. The words 'mouth', 'tongue' and 'voice' occur nine times through the book, more if 'kiss' and 'embrace' are counted, and the word 'blood' (admittedly both as energy source and as blood spilt) six times. The body is constantly there in the poetry's language, both because Al-Raddi holds the vulnerable warmths of human reality key and because hunger counters exile and, just maybe, palliates the spiritual-political abyss that his poetry strives against in the knowledge of likely failure.

Al-Raddi talks about calls at one in the morning that 'climb along the path of the wound'. The wound here is not overtly stated, beyond its being a wound. The poem's title 'Tattoo' gives a hint, but that is not it, nor is it meant to be. The poet means something else. And from the lines:

> Climb toward the source of the wound
> Climb the wound's path till the trail reveals
> The artery's festering wound!

we move through and towards:

> [...] except for the festival between your thighs
> Except for the festival of butterflies and planetary green
> On your coveted back
> The festival – the festival!

and we who read are weighted back to fragile life by remembrance and by strong images that subvert power through tenderness. The aura of 'festival' (the lovely festivals of the body and also the festivals of the public square) is pungent throughout *A Friend's Kitchen*, even if the word itself occurs only four times: Al-Raddi's poetry transforms squares of protest into squares of festivity, making a poetry that is not overtly political but rather – as with much of the best writing – a place where protest, festival, the personal and the political are intertwined and linked inextricably in the language that is given us: a sort of Sufic respite or home. This is what the poet is about in his poetry throughout this collection, saying what he wants to value and know, and what he hopes we may equally come to know and value.

The translations work very well, in part because of the dynamics that exist between the three participants in the translation process. Bryar Bajalan has a strong academic grounding in modern Arabic poetry which has been enriched by a personal working friendship with Al-Raddi, and this is combined in the present book with real creative intuition in his work with his co-translator, the poet Shook, that dates back to shared projects while both were living in northern Iraq. Shook also brings to the work their structural insights of having worked across many languages, as both co-translator and publisher (including inter alia Indigenous languages of Mexico, but also of other poetries in the wider Africa). All of this has combined to focus the translation on place, with its solidities and frailties, and at the same time on boundaries of fracture and abyss, and allows these qualities of Al-Raddi's Arabic – of being both inside and outside at the same time – to shine through in the translation.

This in itself should be enough to recommend this poetry to the English-language reader, but of course there is more: the final poem in the collection, 'From The Book Of Erasure', is another eight-liner in three sections (3/2/3) delivering us to the apparent closure of its three final lines: 'I will narrate nothing / I am busy sweeping away all traces of my existence / Nothing will be left!' But the Sufi in Al-Saddiq Al-Raddi will not let it go at the realities of that but would teach us otherwise, as we furl back to lines in earlier poems: 'Still alive, my body in the river'; 'the dervish was naked / beneath the tunic of longing'; or 'A tongue emerges to sip from the mouth of the abyss'.

Entirely beyond presence and respect, Al-Saddiq Al-Raddi is quite simply a tremendous poet whose lucid and assured work allows us much needed sight into what it perhaps is 'to be someone else'.

Stephen Watts, Whitechapel, 2023

Al-Saddiq Al-Raddi is one of the leading African poets writing in Arabic today. Famous since a teenager, he is admired for the lyric intensity of his poetry and for his principled opposition to Sudan's dictatorship. He is the author of three collections in Arabic: *Songs of Solitude* (1996), *The Sultan's Labyrinth* (1996) and *The Far Reaches of the Screen...* (1999 & 2000); these were published as a single-volume *Collected Poems* in 2010. In 2007 he set up the website Sudanese Ink, a showcase for writers from Sudan and beyond.

Al-Raddi's poems in English translation have been published in *Poetry Review* and the *Times Literary Supplement*, among others. His landmark poem 'Poem of the Nile' was published in the *London Review of Books* and later added to the permanent collection of London's Petrie Museum of Egyptian Archaeology, where Al-Raddi spent time as poet-in-residence during the summer of 2012.

A distinguished journalist and one-time cultural editor of the *Al-Sudani* newspaper, Al-Raddi was forced into exile in 2012 and now lives in London.

Photo by Deellan Khanaka   Photo by Travis Elborough   Photo by Andres Mora

Bryar Bajalan is a writer, translator and filmmaker currently pursuing a doctorate in Arabic and Islamic Studies at the University of Exeter. His work has appeared in *Ambit*, *Hyperallergic* and *Modern Poetry in Translation* among others. His short documentary about early 20th-century Baghdadi poet al-Zahawi won an award for outstanding achievement at the Tagore International Film Festival.

Shook is a poet, translator and editor whose work has spanned a wide range of languages and places. Winner of the 2021 Words Without Borders-Academy of American Poets Poems in Translation Contest for their work with poet Conceição Lima, their most recent translations include the Kurdish iconoclast Farhad Pirbal's *Refugee Number 33,333*, co-translated with Pshtiwan Kamal Babakir.

Stephen Watts is a poet and translation activist whose most recent book is *Journeys Across Breath: Poems 1975–2005* (Prototype, 2022). His *Bibliography Of C20th & C21st Poetries In English Translation* was the subject of the exhibition 'Explosion Of Words' in 2021 with the Swiss artist Hannes Schupbach.

About the Poetry Translation Centre

Set up in 2004, the Poetry Translation Centre is the only UK organisation dedicated to translating, publishing and promoting contemporary poetry from Africa, Asia, the Middle East and Latin America. We introduce extraordinary poets from around the world to new audiences through books, online resources and bilingual events. We champion diversity and representation in the arts and forge enduring relations with diaspora communities in the UK. We explore the craft of translation through our long-running programme of workshops which are open to all.

The Poetry Translation Centre is based in London and is an Arts Council National Portfolio organisation. To find out more about us, including how you can support our work, please visit: www.poetrytranslation.org.

About the World Poet Series

The *World Poet Series* offers an introduction to some of the world's most exciting contemporary poets in an elegant pocket-sized format. The books are presented as dual-language editions, with the English and original-language text displayed side by side. They include specially commissioned translations and completing each book is an afterword essay by an English-language poet, responding to the translations.